T0354426

The *Secret*

Of **Life**

THE LITTLE BOOK THAT CHANGED THE WORLD

REV. AND DR. ROBERT S. LOVE
DR. AMANDA LOVE
DR. SHANNON MARTIN

BALBOA.PRESS
A DIVISION OF HAY HOUSE

Balboa Press books may be ordered through booksellers or by contacting:

Balboa Press
A Division of Hay House
1663 Liberty Drive
Bloomington, IN 47403
www.balboapress.com
1 (877) 407-4847

Because of the dynamic nature of the Internet, any web addresses or
links contained in this book may have changed since publication and
may no longer be valid. The views expressed in this work are solely those
of the author and do not necessarily reflect the views of the publisher,
and the publisher hereby disclaims any responsibility for them.

The author of this book does not dispense medical advice or prescribe the use
of any technique as a form of treatment for physical, emotional, or medical
problems without the advice of a physician, either directly or indirectly. The
intent of the author is only to offer information of a general nature to help
you in your quest for emotional and spiritual well-being. In the event you use
any of the information in this book for yourself, which is your constitutional
right, the author and the publisher assume no responsibility for your actions.

Any people depicted in stock imagery provided by Getty Images are
models, and such images are being used for illustrative purposes only.
Certain stock imagery © Getty Images.

Print information available on the last page.

ISBN: 978-1-9822-3786-8 (sc)
ISBN: 978-1-9822-3787-5 (hc)
ISBN: 978-1-9822-3788-2 (e)

Library of Congress Control Number: 2019917321

Balboa Press rev. date: 11/11/2019

"I'm sorry, I didn't have time to write you a short letter, so I've written a long one instead."
–*Twain*
(or Voltaire or Pascal)

It's short, on purpose.

CONTENTS

CHAPTER 1

The Secret of Life:

Imagine you were placed on this Earth-
no cities, no cars, no roads.

The Secret of Life is a lens. A filter. A framework through which you view and discuss and dissect everything in life. Every decision. Every question. The Secret of Life is a paradigm. Seeing every thought through our lens or paradigm is how we turn information into wisdom. It begins and roots every thought and conversation in the simplest of truths. Knowing this secret and viewing the world through it is like putting on Secret-Formula-Glasses – it lets you see "the matrix": the truth behind the illusion in front of you.

Imagine, just imagine for a second-that you were placed on this Earth-no cities, no cars (planes, trains, etc), no roads. What would you eat? How would you move? What would you know or think?

This is the truth of your physical existence. This is the starting point of understanding you. It does not matter whether or not you believe that God put you here or that you evolved from a lizard or a monkey or a fish. The truth of the physical you is that you are of this Earth. As such, there are rules to existing on this Earth; some can be bent, some can be influenced, and some must simply be followed. Knowing the rules and how to cooperate with some and influence others can allow you to live the life of your dreams.

So-here you are-just you-on Earth. A beautiful, bountiful Earth! (For the purpose of this discussion, this is not a barren waste land, and let's leave predators out of the picture for a minute. Think about a luscious garden forest.). How do you move about? What do you eat? What are you thinking? What do you KNOW? What are the truths of your existence? What is health? What is success? What is worship? What is joyful? If you have a sensation, or a symptom, what does it mean?

You see, this is the truth of you. Many of us born in today's society think that other rules apply. We think that the world is as it is and we are born into it. We accept the status of cities and technology and drugs and politics and religion as truths because that is what we have been born into, but in REALITY, these are all human creations; they are not truths, per say, when it comes to the basic simplest truth of us.

You are a Soul,
Expressing and Experiencing yourself
through a Nervous System,
Running a Body.

You are an incredible, magnificent being on so many levels. There is no shortage of areas to be absolutely amazed at and dazzled by when we take a look at ourselves. Your body is a self-healing, self-regulating, self-organizing eco-organism. You see-when the sperm met the egg for the very first time, in that very moment was a flash of light (Google it), and boom-you became you. From that very instant of fertilization, <u>every bit of information</u> that was necessary to form you into the being that you are now, at this very moment, reading this, was present.

The entirety of innate intelligence, the blueprints for cell, muscle, organ, bone, teeth and brain development-the instructions for how to take ingredients supplied from food and biochemically turn them into what the body needs-EVERYTHING was present in that very first moment. How to breathe and exchange oxygen and carbon dioxide. How to reproduce. Everything-in that one cell. And from that one cell, you divided. You multiplied. Cells <u>were not</u> ADDED to you; you CREATED them yourself. In fact, you have taken from your environment and created every cell that has ever been a part of you-every skin cell, every blood cell, every breath molecule. You are INCREDIBLE! Your design is adaptably PERFECT!

And in that same way, you came with instructions! But I bet you've never read them (kinda like your smartphone)! Don't feel bad, not many people have; however, you are missing out on a bunch of really cool features of you (and probably of your smartphone). If you will live according to your instructions, your design gets to be expressed more completely, more perfectly. Keep close to the design, remove interferences to its expression and watch the richness of life and living unfold like magic! The closer you get, the better it gets! The quality of your reality is directly proportional to the quality of energy that you have available to bring to it. The more energy, the higher the health state, and the better your life. When living in cooperation with your design, there's a richness to life and living that unfolds into your daily existence unlike anything you've ever experienced! There's an energy that's nothing short of magical!

When we stop and read the instructions, we find out just how cool being human is. I mean, let's face it: being born a human in this day and age is like hitting the lotto jackpot! While the world has its problems, there has never been a better time to be alive with more potential. If you know how to look through the lens of the most basic truth of you and apply that knowledge to your life and its circumstances, you have the opportunity to approximate towards the most fulfilled experience your current expression is capable of having. <u>Live in harmony (or as close as you can) with how we are made and you will feel the energy richness that is your birth right!</u>

And one of the best parts is, there's no time that you can't make a change and head in the direction of your optimal innate expression. You see, your body is basically an energized recycling dump. You take energy and nutrients from the environment, create new cells, discard old cells, and continually repeat this cycle. A quick look at your hands will reveal this: they're not anything like your hands five years ago. In fact, that's completely accurate; there's not a single cell in them that is the same as five years ago. Five years from now, they will be different again. Your body goes through 99% complete cellular turnover approximately every two years. So, every few years, you literally have a chance to grow an entirely new body, with entirely different cells, based on how well you can follow the design.

So-take every decision and look at it through the lens of *"You, on this Earth, no cities, no cars, no roads."* What would you eat? Loosely: raw plant-based, organic foods: vegetables, fruits, seeds, nuts, and you would pay attention to how certain amounts of those foods made you feel. Probably some limited amounts of meat at certain times, but again, filter it through the lens-the meat would be pasture raised and grass fed mostly, or fresh caught from a non-contaminated water source. It's what would be available to you. You can filter every food you eat through this lens to see if it is compatible with your design.

What would you drink? Water. Maybe you'd put something in your water, but generally, water. These are the things your body is designed to consume. It's literally part of your blueprint. Your body THRIVES under these conditions because it is how you are designed and built to thrive as part of life on Earth. This is how you get the appropriate building blocks to build healthy new cells and tissues according to your blueprint-by having a <u>sufficient amount</u> of what IS needed, and not too much of what is not.

How would you move? By foot. Maybe on a horse or an elephant if you can befriend one. You would walk or run or hike-everywhere. You would also do this mostly barefoot or with a soft foot covering, and on soft ground, not concrete. What is the first thing an animal (think dog, cat) does when it wakes up? It stretches! So would you-you would stretch out, check in with your body and alignment. You are designed to stretch, to be aware, to move a certain amount-your cells and tissues depend on it.

So again, apply the filter-do you move like a human should? Do your shoes support a natural human movement? Are you walking at least 30 minutes a day? Do you have at least a beginner's level body awareness? Stretching, motion? Spinal health? The spine houses the nervous system-the communication system between the brain and body, the interface between your consciousness and the world-it needs to have fluid movement for it to work at 100%. Does yours? Are you missing part of the experience of your environment because your spine is stuck and signals cannot be sent and received appropriately?

How would you think? If you have access to everything you basically need, and you are not in lack or starvation, life would generally be as you see it. Would you observe nature? Would you lie under the stars at night and think about the universe? Even in tribal times up to not so long ago, it would have been entirely normal for a human to go their entire life and never have even heard of the concept of a murder. Much of our environmental stresses today are self-imposed. The news serves us all our bad news daily (24/7/365), but in reality, roughly 7.1 billion people were good people all day yesterday and made the world a nice place to be! Would you seek relationship with the Divine? Where would you seek? How would you seek? Stillness, conversation, meditation, prayer?

These are the basic truths of your physical existence. And while our modern world has done some things to make life harder (news, poisoning oceans, bad agricultural practices), the modern world has also made it the easiest it has ever been, in the history of Earth, to coordinate and source and build your own luscious garden forest congruent life. You have the ability to get fresh (or fresh frozen) organic food year-round from anywhere in the world. You have the ability to source good healthy meats. You're not limited to what is available just around you seasonally or agriculturally. We have the ability to order footwear which mimics natural walking even though many of us live in a concrete jungle.

We have access to the whole of human knowledge at our fingertips regularly. We can read and learn and grow from any wisdom tradition, meditation, different religious tradition, different culture in ways that were not available even only a few years ago. We can network and communicate. We can see the good all around the world at any time. With the internet available to us, we can choose our content and our programming, we are not just at the mercy of television and news programming anymore!

If you will apply this lens to your life and decisions, you will bear witness to a dramatic shift in your energy-richness! You will begin to experience the fullness of life! You will see health and vibrancy and vitality surge in all aspects of your being! You are beautifully and wonderfully designed and made, and it is high time you get to experience it! Remove the interferences, and give all the ingredients, and watch the magnificence of your life unfold!

In the coming months and years, hundreds, perhaps even thousands of pages will be written to further explore the application and use of this lens, but the lens itself is right here in these foundational first pages. Apply it. Apply it to your life-how and what you eat, how you move, how and what you think. Apply it to science and how we research and ask questions. Apply it to energy and waste and recycling. Apply it to relationships and health decisions and spirituality. Apply it to politics, to community relations. Look through the lens at everything and watch everything change.

In our never-ending quest of self-awareness, this lens provides a compass to guide your way. Along the journey, you may have to dodge a tree or ford a river, but you will know what true north is. There may be other work required of you to engage and embrace your full self. You may have to search the various wisdom traditions and spiritual teachings to also get in touch with your Soul, your Consciousness. You may have to work on mastering control of your state of being and influencing your physiology to match your needs or desires (or vice versa). You may have to learn to become aware of your body AND your Energetic Self through breath, presence, stillness or through loud noises and movement! Keep learning!

A quick note about Perfection: In this book, we are going to give you information based on ideals and perfect circumstances. Your life may or may not always allow you to line up with everything in this book. Perfectionism can be its own curse. While pursuing these ideals perfectly is an awesome ambition, the realities of life commonly will not allow for this. Your goal is Progress. Progress trumps Perfection – every time! Pursuing and deploying the wisdom from this book a little bit at a time, in any way that you can, is a win. Creating opportunities for short-term perfection in the form of retreats, get-aways, or challenges is also great. But know – for most of us, trying to live this information perfectly, all of the time, is unsustainable. Do not beat yourself up over it. You can never undo the consequence of a good choice. Make all of the good choices that you can. No bad choice can undo the benefits of a good choice, so don't get hung up, just keep moving forward.

Live your journey to its fullest! Love where you are! Head in the direction of where you want to be! Imagine a life where every day gets better, where you live energy-rich, where you live disease-free, and where you always bring the best version of yourself to your family, friends, and daily life! You are the lead explorer of your life-dive in and uncover and unlock the mysteries of living your fullest expression of physical and spiritual, of body, mind and soul!

CHAPTER 2

Divine Food

"You are what you eat."-Old Proverb

However you came to be here, (God/Universal Intelligence/ Flying Spaghetti Monster/Big Bang), you are here and there is a grand organizing design and force in place orchestrating everything from the spin of atoms to the spin of galaxies. Henceforth in this book, we will refer to this intelligence, design, entity as Source. You may put whatever moniker in place that you like, we just need something to help us move forward together in discussion.

Source put you here and gave you everything you need in exactly the form congruent with your design. (And not only that, but designed you to contribute back into the whole ecosystem too. Food goes in, fertilizer comes out).

The perfect diet for humans can be found by applying the same lens that we will apply to everything else. So let's start from the top: Imagine yourself placed on this Earth, no cities, no cars, no roads. What do you eat? Or, better yet – would you eat "this"? You can ask this question of literally everything that you consume, everything you see in a grocery store, or everything you read on a restaurant menu. "Would I eat this in nature?" Eating congruently with our design sets the foundation for sufficiency, adaptability, a life free of disease and full of energy.

If you were placed on this Earth in your very own Garden of Eden, you would walk and roam to find the freshest, most ripe fruits, vegetables, nuts, seeds, and berries available. You would most likely consume them in the raw form that they come in. The time from vine-to-mouth would be minimal. They would certainly be organic, and not covered and coated in toxic pesticides. The way that you eat today should mimic this model.

What we know from modern life science, paired with archeology and forensic science, is that our human genetic code has not changed hardly at all in thousands of years. In fact, it has changed less than 0.0001% in 5,000 years. What that has allowed us to see is a pretty good picture of what our changing environment has done to our health and disease profiles, even as our genes have not changed. The conversations that have arisen as a result of these studies have led to a whole new appreciation of the science of epigenetics. The combination of all of these perspectives is what has allowed us to gather a view of what a diet perfect for humans looks like according to our genetic profile.

What you need most is sufficiency. You need a sufficient (or more than sufficient) amount of all of the minerals, micronutrients, and phytochemicals required by your genetic code on a daily basis, in their raw form, in order to make healthy cells and tissues. This is what your genetic code calls for and expects. Nature delivers food as a nutrient complex, not as isolated vitamins and minerals. In the whole of science, even today, we have not been able to even list all of the cofactors available in our basic fruits and vegetables. Source put them there, in perfect order, with your design, for your consumption and success! And, that is how they are meant to be consumed: in their raw form, with all cofactors present and intact. Furthermore, your nutrient and ingredient storage levels determine your cellular health and adaptability.

If you are deficient in any one or more minerals, micronutrients, or phytochemicals, your body CANNOT produce completely healthy cells and tissues. The bottom line is – if you don't have the ingredients, you cannot make the recipe! Your genetic code contains the recipe; what you put in your mouth and in what form gives the ingredients. Now, your body is INCREDIBLY adaptable and you can survive on substitutions and adaptations, but they come at a cost-that cost is illness and disease. Many humans survive 70 years on diet coke and cheeseburgers, but they'll never know the richness, vitality, and expanded lifespan and function that they could have – if they were sufficient!

So, right now, as you read this, all of the cells that compose you are the product of the choices that you have made and the sufficiency/deficiency levels you have maintained over the last 2 or so years. Are your cells sufficient and healthy? Are you experiencing your maximum cellular health and adaptability?

Or, is it likely that you are producing substandard cells with substitutions instead of real ingredients? Can you imagine what life will look like after a complete round of cellular turnover with sufficient ingredients to build fully healthy cells, according to your Source-given design?

Our modern agricultural practices have created a double-edged sword. On the beneficial side, there has never been a better time in the history of humanity for you to have the availability of the full spectrum of nutrients that your body needs than now. However, on the detrimental side, many of our agricultural processes have inadvertently depleted our food of the nutrients that they should normally contain and have also added toxins, which we were never meant to consume. While pesticides and GMO's have supported large agricultural undertakings, there is no doubt that they are having a significant effect on our toxic load. And, if you have ever placed a tomato from a conventional grocery store, beside an heirloom tomato bought from a farmer's market, beside a home-grown or farm tomato and tasted the difference, you would immediately recognize – through taste – the robust nutrient difference between the three. Our modern farming practices often do not allow food to ripen, has our food spending an extended amount of time in cold storage between harvesting and arriving at the grocery store, and almost always coats our food in toxic pesticides. These factors, and more, result in food that is deplete in nutrients that are supposed to naturally be there and are instead coated in toxins. Furthermore, if you cook your fruits and vegetables,

13

you further lose nutrients. And microwaves destroy nutrients almost entirely. And, so far – we've only talked about produce.

Going back to the beneficial side of modern agriculture, there has never been more accessibility to organic and locally-grown food – in the history of man. Organic food is grown without pesticides (or mostly without pesticides) and locally grown food is far more likely to be vine-ripened and contains the nutrients of your local soil, which is part of your ecosystem and local environment. Pair this with the rising popularity of online delivery and/or pick-up options, co-ops, and health-conscious meal-prep services, you literally have the ability to create your own Garden of Eden in your house 24/7/365.

Because agriculture has changed the way that our food is grown and harvested, some of the nutrients that Source put there are not as bioavailable as they should be. However, swinging back to the good side of things, lucky for us – in this day and age – we can take supplements to fill in the gaps. Finding good, whole-food based, full micronutrient-spectrum organic vitamins, omega-3's, and vitamin D – all essential nutrients to our genetic code – is thankfully, a viable option for all of us today. We want to find these in a form as close to their whole, natural form as possible – the way that Source made them. The more isolated, synthetic, or biochemically-derived a supplement is, the more it looks like a substitution, rather than an ingredient, to our genetic code.

Let's talk about meat. There are many moral, ethical, and political reasons not to consume meat, but the reality is – humans have been doing it for thousands of years and our genetic code responds to it. The meat that our ancestors ate, however, is vastly different from the conventional commercial meat that we are consuming today. All of the meat that our ancestors ate was grass-fed, antibiotic-free, hormone-free, free-range meat. Our modern meat farming practices have dramatically changed the nutritional value of the meat that we eat today. From the added hormones and antibiotics, to the altered omega-6 levels, today's meat is drastically different from the way Source originally designed it. Also worth noting – for a human, a sufficient amount of meat, in its whole form, is approximately 7 ounces per day, which is a portion about the size of an iPhone.

When it comes to finding good-quality sources of meat these days, we are fortunate to have options; however, we have to be diligent in our selection. Bison and free-range chicken are the best commonly-available commercial options. Almost all other forms of modern meat suffer from the modern agricultural process. Every deviation from the animal living in a different way than Source intended it to, results in an alteration of the tissue make-up of the animal, and therefore of the meat that we eventually consume. How the animal is harvested affects the hormones that are coursing through its muscles, which become what we consume. When we consume meat from sick and scared animals, it changes our composition too. Almost all commercial chicken operations – even cage-free operations – dramatically change the natural life and make-up of a chicken. Modern industrial cattle farming relies on drugs and grain-finishing to create our beef supply, all of which are unnatural processes for cows. Nearly all of the fish in the ocean carry some amount of mercury, PCB toxicity, or radiation. Again, the question becomes: How closely was this animal allowed to live in the way Source intended? The further from the design, the greater the consequence to our health.

Are you eating food, or food-like products? Many of the products that have made our lives convenient hold no actual nutritional value. Most packaged foods, while convenient, are calorie-rich and nutrient-poor. Our bodies, being highly adaptable, can take energy from them, and can try to make the most of it, but are still left nutrient-deficient and nutrient-seeking. There is a distinct difference between calories and nutrients. Calories will give us energy, but nutrients are what gives us the ingredients to build our cells. If we are lacking in certain nutrients, our bodies will make a sub-par version of our cells using substitutions, which then makes it impossible to create 100% healthy tissue.

Unfortunately, our modern agricultural processes have not only created a multitude of products which perpetuate this problem but accompanying science and corporate greed have actually made it worse. There is an entire field of study built around the science of satiation. Many of today's products are scientifically designed to take you just below your point of satisfaction, so that you enjoy it, but that you also still want more. This idea gives new meaning to the old catch-phrase "Bet you can't eat just one!".

Nearly 80% of processed foods contain MSG. MSG has more than 50 different names. It excites brain fat-programs and is used exclusively to create obesity in lab mice. Similarly, nearly all packaged foods contain high-fructose corn syrup. High-fructose corn syrup is an isolated, super-concentrated, refined sugar. It is the crack-cocaine of sugars. High fructose corn syrup has more than 10 different names. It is 100% fat-free, but it stimulates your insulin response to directly produce fat. The bottom line: there are no food-like products or packaged products found in nature. The more pre-packaged, modified, boxed, or "more-ingredients-on-the-label" something is, the greater the consequence to your health.

Speaking of things that are fat-free, diet soda is not your friend. Diet soda will deliver a momentary biochemical change in the brain. A combination of aspartame and caffeine create an excitotoxin, which causes a momentarily pleasurable buzz or high before causing cell death. Most sugar-free products or sweetening sugar substitutes are highly biochemically-derived and come with serious health consequences to their consumption.

All fluffy carbohydrates become sugar in the body and the bloodstream. Sugar is a drug that gets you high. It has been scientifically demonstrated to be more addictive than cocaine.

In addition to all of the places that sugar is lurking in your food in the form of isolates like high fructose corn syrup, all of the following are pure sugar once they enter your digestive system:

bread

bagels

pasta

cereal

wheat

rice

white potatoes

corn

waffles

pancakes

crackers

cookies

cakes

muffins

oats

pita bread

wraps

grains

whole grains

macaroni and cheese

Chex

potato chips

corn chips

anything breaded, battered and/or fried

Even things that we don't think contain sugar usually have added sugar, including salad dressings and condiments (even most commercial soy sauces have a higher wheat content than soy). Almost all dairy contains sugar or causes a blood sugar spike. If you want to visualize how much sugar is in milk, Jamie Oliver gave a TED talk where he demonstrated that each carton of milk that an elementary school child receives at school each day has as much sugar as a can of soda and then proceeded to show you that they will consume an entire wheelbarrow of sugar just from their school milk, from their elementary school years alone.

The bottom line here: sugar is lurking in products and forms that you would never expect, and it is almost impossible to keep up with its many names in modern food production, but The Secret of Life makes it easy for you. You don't have to remember a list; all that you have to ask is: "If I were walking through my luscious garden forest, would this be available in a natural form that I would eat? Would I ever walk through a field of wheat and break off a stalk to chew on? Would I ever walk through a rice patty and pick up a handful of rice to eat?" If you cannot pick it up and eat it without requiring processing and modification, then it was not meant for you to eat in the first place.

Similarly, many other seemingly natural products, like dairy, are not actually very natural. Even in its raw, natural form, milk from an animal is meant for that specific animal and not for humans. Cow's milk is for baby cows. Goat's milk is for baby goats. Humans make their own milk, as it turns out. It's called breastmilk, and it's made for baby humans.

This departure from our natural way of being, paired with the emergence of drive-through fast food has ushered in an epidemic of obesity in the United States from the 1980's to the present. The USA has gotten fatter every year for more than 40 years. In 1980, there was not a single state with a measurable obesity problem. Today, more than half of all Americans are overweight or obese. At any given moment, 1/3rd of US Women and ¼ of US Men are on a diet. Despite this, more than half of them will gain back more than they lose in the 12 months following their program. Furthering this problem, many people do not understand that their body encapsulates heavy metal toxins in fat. Many times, the body will not allow you to burn that fat unless you have the proper cofactors present to safely facilitate the elimination of these toxins from your body. Lots of people just can't lose that "last five pounds" around their midsection; they may not understand that they need to add nutrients so that their body has what is required to process the heavy metal toxins that are contained within that last five pounds.

We have to stop dieting and instead learn to understand what our Diet is: the collection of what and how humans as a species should eat. Eating a Divine diet will allow your body to approach its natural, healthy set-point in weight while simultaneously promoting healthy organs, tissues, and skin. You may lose weight (or gain weight), according to your specific natural design.

So, specifically, what *should* you eat? Fruits, vegetables, raw nuts, raw seeds, and meat – all as close to their natural, divine, Source-given design as possible. If you can eat them raw, that is the best way. In terms of fruits and vegetables, "Eat the Rainbow!" The more naturally colorful your plate or bowl is, the better it likely is for you. When you're cooking meat or vegetables, cook them slowly, at low-temperatures, and consume the juice and/or broth that they are cooked in, so that they retain as many nutrients as possible. Every time you heat something up, you lose some nutrient value (because you are modifying it from its natural design).

We recommend utilizing modern technology to help you eat raw foods in new and exciting ways. Food processors, juicers, and blenders, particularly the Vitamix, provide excellent ways to enjoy ample raw foods. Fruit and berry smoothies are an excellent way to nutrient-load as are vegetable juices. Juicing and blending allow us to consume larger quantities of nutrients, in their raw form, then if we had to sit and eat them in their raw form off of a plate.

We further recommend that each day, you consume one Super Salad and a seven-ounce portion of good-quality meat, such as slow-cooked, free-range chicken, or bison. There are ample recipes available online for juices, smoothies, salads, and incredible raw food meals. For your convenience, we have included just a few of our favorite recipes below, including the Super Salad:

Super Salad

Spring Mix

Sprouts

Tomato

Cucumber

3-4 Tops of Broccoli

3-4 Tops of Cauliflower

Carrots

Celery

¼ Yellow Pepper

¼ Red Pepper

¼ Green Pepper

¼ Orange Pepper

Beets

Zucchini/Squash

Onion (Fresh)

Avocado

Smoothies

1 Banana

6-10 Whole Strawberries

2-4 Pitted Dates

4 oz Almond or Coconut Milk

Scoop of Ice

1 Banana

1 Cup Berries (Blueberry, Raspberry, Blackberry)

2-4 Pitted Dates

4 oz Almond or Coconut Milk

Fruit Juices

Apple-Orange

2 Apples
1 Orange

Black Pineapple

1 Cup Blackberries
2 Spears Pineapple
½ Cup Blueberries
½ Cup Raspberries
Sprigs of Parsley

Strawberry Mint

1/2 large Pineapple
1 Cup Strawberries
1 Pear
Mint leaves

Blackberry Kiwi

1/4 large Pineapple
1 Cup Blackberries
1-2 Kiwifruit
1 Pear

Cherry Sunrise

1 Cup pitted Cherries
1 Grapefruit
1 Apple

Cranberry

1 Cup Cranberries
1 Cup Grapes
¼ large Pineapple

Eye Opener

2 Cups Strawberries
2 Carrots
1 Orange

Star Berry

2 Star Fruits
1 Cup Blackberries
½ Cup Blueberries
½ Cup Raspberries

Summer Nectar

3 Nectarines, pitted
2 Apricots, pitted
1 Cup Blueberries
2 Peaches, pitted
2 Plums, pitted

CHAPTER 3

Water

> "What's amazing about water is that it is able
> to show us myriad 'faces' depending upon the
> condition it is in or the information it is given."
> – Masaru Emoto

You are comprised of somewhere between 70-90% water. Knowing this fact, it may be of great value to us to think about our water and its importance in our lives. Returning to our basic premise: Imagine yourself, placed on this earth, no cities, no cars, no roads; what would you drink? Water. What else would be available? Where would you find it, and what form would it be in? The most common source would be a fresh stream, where the water has been filtered and mineralized naturally over the rocks. The second most common place would be a well, where the same is true. This is not the reality of the water that we find around us today.

Today's running water sources do provide us with incredible hygiene options: indoor plumbing, toilets, and fresh-water bathing options are luxuries that have helped to eradicate diseases and improve health outcomes. However, it has come at a cost: that cost is the level of processing that it takes, and the chemicals added as a result of that process. Tap water today, most notably including the water that you shower in, is loaded with chlorine, fluoride, heavy metal toxins and hormone and drug residue that our current municipal filtering systems cannot remove. The ill-effects of these added chemicals have been seen in multiple studies, which has led to the modern rise in filtration options. Most notably, when you shower or bathe in steaming water, these chemicals can be inhaled. If you cannot have a whole house filter, it is important to – at the very least – have a filter on each shower head that you and your family use in order to minimize these inhaled toxins.

When it comes to drinking water, the same is true of tap water. We are meant to drink approximately half of our body weight in ounces of water per day. Some of that count may come from the fresh, raw, fruits and vegetables that we consume, but it needs to be mostly from the water that we consume. There are a variety of filtration options available to us – some are better than others. Most common filters do not remove heavy metal toxins or fluoride. Your best bet is either reverse osmosis or distilled water. We recommend that you invest in one of these filtration systems for your home – or, at the very least, for your kitchen so that the water you drink and cook with is safe.

Bottled water has become readily available to us in modern society – but it is not without its costs. The environmental effects, not to mention the health effects, of plastic water bottles cannot be ignored or denied. In addition, not all bottled waters are created equal. If you choose to drink bottled water for the convenience, please research the various brands for their purity and impact on the environment. There are several third-party agencies which rank the quality of bottled water every year; some of the most well-known brands on earth, with excellent marketing to make us trust them, are not much better than the tap water you can get from your kitchen sink. One particularly well-known brand is harvested from the gorgeous island springs that they claim to be harvested from, then put into large, plastic drums in container ships that are then sent to China for bottling. This allows the water to potentially sit for weeks along the journey, which may contaminate the amazing, fresh, spring water that you think that you are getting.

In an ideal world, you would carry your water with you throughout the day in a glass or steel container, refilled at a RO (reverse osmosis) or spring water source. Ideally, you would not drink water 30 minutes before or during your meals. You would sip your water throughout the day; you are not a camel and have no water storage mechanism. There are, however, some ways to help your body retain some water and process it differently, naturally. Gelatinous fibers, such as aloe, chia seeds, and coconut meats allow your body to slowly process water. They create a fat-soluble binding process as it moves through your body, which is particularly helpful for organ hydration. These substances (and other water-rich, raw fruits and vegetables eaten throughout the day) allow for a better up-take of water throughout our tissues, mimicking how our bodies would process water if we existed more in line with our Source-given design.

Your body is incredibly adaptable, as we know. Most humans are chronically dehydrated and will never even consciously realize it. There have been incredible studies in alteration of disease profiles and visible skin changes in humans across 30 days simply by creating proper hydration in their lives.

Think about all of your cells right now. Based on your last two years of daily water consumption, how hydrated are your cells? Think about how vastly different your cellular makeup will be after two years of sufficient hydration! You have so much to look forward to!

While you may think that you can tell your level of dehydration by the color of your urine (which is often actually true), true hydration/dehydration is a cellular function and can only be seen in bloodwork, under a microscope. It can take your body up to one month (and sometimes longer) to properly hydrate with adequate daily intake of clean, refreshing water. Basically, anything that you drink that is not water (soda, commercial juice, coffee, tea) is contributing to your dehydration.

CHAPTER 4

Nerve Function & Nerve System

"Every system and function in your body is
controlled by the one under your hat."
-adapted from BJ Palmer

The Nervous System is the Master Control System of your body. It controls and coordinates every other system, organ, muscle, tissue, cell, and signal. The brain and spinal cord comprise the Central Nervous System, or your Central Operating Computer, while the nerves themselves make up the communication pathways over which signals are sent and received between that Central System and every other part of YOU. It runs everything, gives you every sensation, and turns every thought into action.

It is the interface between the nonphysical you and the physical you. It's where thoughts become actions and sensations become thoughts. It controls all of your functions, most especially your organs – most of which you cannot actually feel. It gives you the ability to perceive every emotion, every feeling, every sensation. The nervous system is the seat of Consciousness. If you seek to be awakened, enlightened, and more connected with Source and/or the Field, then the state of your nervous system is of the utmost importance, both in its transmission ability, efficiency, and coherence.

You experience your entire life in your Central Nervous System – and nowhere else. For example, if I were to poke you in the finger with a pin, you would tell me that you felt that pin-prick in your finger. This is an illusion. If I were to cut the sensory nerve in your arm between your finger and your Central Nervous System and proceed to poke you in the finger with that pin, you would not experience the pain at all. You would not feel a thing – even though the pin-prick is still happening. You only have experiences in your Central Nervous System – your Master Control System. This system's ability to send and receive information can be interfered with in multiple ways.

That interference can cause loss of function. That interference can cause altered perception. That interference can cause decreased processing power. In many of these examples, you will be completely unaware that you are being affected unless you are regularly measuring your nervous system using technology that can alert you to its state-because much of this you cannot consciously feel. The percentage of function and adaptability you have in your nervous system is like the percentage gauge of how much potential processing power you have for your life.

Interference can come in multiple forms and be caused by multiple factors. Physical, chemical, emotional, and mental stressors can create interference to the function of the nervous system. The simplest example that we can give you is this: if you slip and fall and knock a bone out of place in your back, it can put mechanical pressure on a nerve and alter that nerve's ability to send and receive signals between the brain and the body dramatically.

If you ingest certain toxins, your body may respond with a hormone cascade that interferes with the nervous system's ability to send and receive signals. If you ingest or encounter certain other toxins, your body may encapsulate them and store them in the dorsal horn of the spinal cord and purposely block that part of your nervous system off from function in order to protect the rest of your body from those toxins. If you happen to acquire a toxic load over years and years, this same thing may be true. Incredible research is being explored currently related to heavy metal toxicity in our bodies acquired over a lifetime. It's not a problem until the load reaches a certain level. Examples of this can include mercury poisoning from leaking fillings in your teeth or aluminum poisoning from deodorant.

Your Nervous System has two "modes". Parasympathetic and Sympathetic. You should remember these from high school health class at some point. You may know them better as Rest and Digest (Parasympathetic) and Fight or Flight (Sympathetic). When your Master Control System is in either of these two modes, it responds and coordinates the rest of the body according to that mode's needs. We humans are meant to spend 80% or more of our life and daily time in Rest and Digest (Parasympathetic). Most of us do not. But again, think about us-put on this planet, no cities, no cars, no roads. What does life look like for us as a tribal people? Wake up with the sunrise, commune with the tribe, forage or hunt for some food, build and fellowship with the tribe, eat, fire, celebrate, prepare for sleep as you gaze at the star-filled sky. Pretty chill. Pretty parasympathetic.

Fight or Flight mode is part of our design that makes a lot of sense for our code hundreds and thousands of years ago. It would only kick-in in the event of an emergency. However, our modern life and world isn't what it was when our code was designed and developed. Fight or Flight is brilliant when you're running away from a tiger or bear in the woods, or if you're warring with the neighboring tribe next door. Fight or Flight mode changes your entire physiology for battle or fleeing. What that means is that it is going to shut down or down-regulate any system that is non-essential to survival in the moment. Digestion is not important when you're running from a tiger. Reproduction is not important when you're facing a bear in the woods. Immune system function is not essential when you are fleeing for your life. Clotting factors increase in Fight or Flight because your body is preparing for a potential wound. Blood pressure and heart rate go up and stay up. You get the Fight or Flight hormone cascade of Cortisol, Epinephrine and Norepinephrine. Your adrenals fire. Your sweat glands activate. Blood flow moves away from extremities and into large muscle groups.

All of these are intelligent adaptations for Fight or Flight, in an actual Fight or Flight scenario; the problem is that your body doesn't know the difference between a tiger and your overdue cell phone bill. Between your boss and a bear. Between traffic and the enemy tribe next door. Your body knows each of these modern stressors just as stressors and responds accordingly.

Let's run through an average day for most people:
1. You wake up to the most obnoxious alarm you can set. Fight or Flight.
2. You leave yourself just barely enough time to get ready and go. Fight or Flight.
3. Traffic. Fight or Flight.
4. Morning Work/School. Fight or Flight.
5. Lunch! Rest and Digest (if you're not stressed out over the morning or upcoming afternoon).
6. Afternoon Work/School. Fight or Flight.
7. Traffic. Fight or Flight.
8. Kids/Shopping/Adult Responsibilities. Fight or Flight.
9. TV! Rest and Digest (if you're not watching Murder, Death, Kill: Special Victims Unit).
10. Attempt to Sleep until pending alarm and next day.

You're spending 90% of your day in Fight or Flight mode. Day In and Day Out. Stress is stress to your body and nervous system, unless and until you upgrade your ability to adapt and process it. One of the largest foundational root cause reasons we are seeing outbreaks of chronic lifestyle disease patterns in modern life is stress. Know someone with digestive problems (IBS, Chron's, Celiac, GERD, Reflux, Constipation)? Are they calm and chill or stressed? Have you seen the statistics on infertility? What percentage of their days and lives are these couples spending in Fight or Flight? Reproduction is not essential when your body thinks you are running from a tiger. Know anyone with chronic muscle aches and headaches that even massages don't help? What mode are they in most of the time? High blood pressure? Same question. Insulin or blood sugar problems? Same question. Cholesterol problems? Same question. Heart Disease, Cancer, Depression, Autoimmune? When we spend all day, every day in Fight or Flight, what else would we expect?

Lastly, when you go into Fight or Flight, your nervous system literally initiates a physical postural response. Have you ever seen a whipped or scared dog or cat? How do they look? Tucked tail? Tucked head? That's because of a mechanism known as adverse mechanical cord tension. Your nerve system will literally pull your spine into a tucked posture. Think about when we cry-are we expanded and open-armed or curled up? Think about a good boxing posture-tucked head, tucked tail. It's our natural physiological response. Except-when we spend an extended amount of time in Fight or Flight, our body literally starts to permanently adopt that posture. Head forward, tailbone tucked, tensioning the whole system. This posture, in and of itself, can cause interference in the nervous system. Adverse Mechanical Cord Tension. When your spine is under tension, it cannot move in its normal range, which literally limits your ability to process and perceive the world around you, or to adapt effectively to it.

So, the key to all of this is ensuring that you have a 100% healthy and interference-free functioning nervous system, 100% of the time. Or at least as close as you can get it! Again, going back to our Source-given design, keeping that system intact and interference-free, in parasympathetic mode as often as possible and with optimum motion, mobility and adaptability.

And that friends, is where good, neurologically-based chiropractic care comes in. Chiropractic is the only profession which has a focus on optimizing your nervous system. Getting under regular care for the purpose of living your optimal life is a lifestyle choice for anyone wanting to grow healthier, enhance performance and/or expand their consciousness. Now, not all chiropractors are created equal. You may have to search through several to find a good one. But please, don't get discouraged if your first or second encounter isn't great. Your nervous system health is worth the search to find a good one.

There are more than 300 techniques in chiropractic designed to help clear the nerve system. They are all effective and have all been studied, although some more than others. Some techniques are better for specific individuals. The main thing is: are they clearing your nervous system of interference, allowing you to function at your best?

And chiropractic doesn't have to be rough or hurt! Techniques have been developed to work directly with the nervous system through gentle, specific touches and adjustments. Torque Release Technique is practiced by thousands of chiropractors around the world. It is gentle, specific and heavily researched. Torque Release Technique has been shown to dramatically change spinal curves via x-ray, improve heart rate variability, change self-reported wellness scores and even help those battling with addictions. It uses an instrument, called the Integrator, which has been approved by the FDA for the adjustment of subluxation. TRT represents one of the quickest, easiest and most gentle ways to restore and optimize your nervous system!

Emerging from chiropractic, there is one technique which has been studied at the highest levels and shown to be able to advance the coherence of the neurospinal system. This means, that beyond simply clearing your nerve system of interference, it also teaches your system to adapt and process at ever-increasing levels of coherence and energy efficiency. To put it simply, keeping your nervous system clear through chiropractic is essential for keeping your Central Operating System running at 100%; but, if you want to upgrade your entire system, you're looking for Network Spinal. Practiced by doctors around the world who have completed post-doctorate training at the highest levels, Network Spinal is at the forefront of consciousness, health, and performance-enhancing studies.

Clearing and upgrading the function of your nervous system is like enhancing your Secret-Formula Glasses. It's one thing to know the Secret of Life, and another thing entirely to be able to see it, perceive it, and take action on it. You can read and know everything in this book, but the health and function of your nervous system is what will dictate your level of perception and awareness, and therefore, your ability to take action and become fully healthy.

We all get our nervous systems evaluated at least weekly, if not daily. There's never a chance that we want to be at less of a percentage than what we have to be. Why would you ever want your nervous system to function at any less, for any extended period of time? It is the single, most important thing that we do and the central piece of our total healthcare regimen.

CHAPTER 5

Digestion & Poop

"Everybody poops."-Old Proverb

The second most important body system to take care of (after your nervous system) is your gut. Digestion and pooping are key to healthy function. Eighty to ninety percent of your immune system is directly controlled or influenced through gut-processes. Digestion is a function of a healthy nervous system, sending and receiving appropriate signals from a healthy gut, digesting and processing divine food.

Unfortunately, as you know from Chapter 2, many of our modern foods are not designed with our health (or gut health) in mind. Every food ingested that is not in its divine form presents a challenge to our gut. Many modern products that we consume without thought actually strip the gut lining and cilia, which are so vital to our ability to digest and assimilate good nutrients. Once our gut lining has been compromised, it makes it hard to digest properly, even when we eat the right foods.

When the cilia and gut lining have been stripped, we often see a condition called "Leaky Gut Syndrome". The purpose of the gut lining is to keep things out of the bloodstream that should not be there (along with keeping things moving throughout the digestive tract). When your gut lining has been stripped and compromised, particles that should not be able to pass through this barrier are able to pass through and enter the bloodstream, causing system inflammation. This is when we begin to see conditions arise like autoimmunity, Chron's Disease, Celiac Disease, Ulcerative Colitis, Diverticulitis, Ulcers, Reflux, GERD, stones, Irritable Bowel Syndrome, and constipation.

Beyond the delicate, natural structures of the gut, there is an entire ecosystem of healthy gut bacteria that are essential to good digestion and good health. This ecosystem is known as your microbiome and is what constitutes much of the immune system in your gut that we mentioned earlier. Not only does this microbiome help to make up your immune system, but they also contribute to creating vitamins right in your own gut! A delicate balance must exist for these functions to occur.

Going back to The Secret of Life: If you were placed on this earth, no cities, no cars, no roads, how would you eat? You would pick raw fruits and vegetables straight from the earth; you would most likely eat them without washing them. At the very most, you would rinse them with water – they would never be scrubbed clean with detergent like we currently do today. Did you know that there is bacteria in the soil (along with minerals) that we are meant to consume? When we scrub our fruits and vegetables clean (which is almost required now-a-days because our produce is covered in pesticides), we are scrubbing away bacteria that help our microbiome thrive. In fact, we consume 1/1,000,000th of the beneficial bacteria that our ancestors did – even if we are doing our best to eat healthy, raw fruits and vegetables every day. In addition to this, we are bombarding our bodies with unnatural chemicals that destroy our microbiome, such as antibiotics, mouthwash and antibacterial soaps and hand sanitizers, and flooding our digestive systems with processed sugars, which causes an overgrowth of "bad" bacteria. This is why it is essential to supplement with probiotics, which are these beneficial bacteria packaged into a supplement form.

Our microbiome requires food and nutrients to stay alive (just like we do!). These food and nutrients are known as prebiotics, which are present in raw fruits and vegetables. Prebiotics allow our gut bacteria to thrive and flourish.

If all things are working correctly in your gut and digestive system, you should poop at least once per day (naturally, without laxatives or other interventions). If this is not the case for you, then you should be aware and begin a conversation with your healthcare provider. Bringing this back to The Secret of Life, pooping today is not like how we were designed to poop. Modern toilets often leave your legs at ninety-degrees and put pressure on the glutes and back-of-the-thigh muscles. Our natural design for pooping involves us squatting much deeper than ninety-degrees with active muscle engagement. A rudimentary knowledge of anatomy reveals that the angle of the bowels and colon changes from the seated to squatting position to allow for easier pooping. One of the greatest recent inventions in pooping and digestive health is the Squatty Potty. Designed to help your body get into a natural pooping position, eliminating strain, while enjoying the conveniences of your modern toilet, the Squatty Potty is a no-brainer investment to move in the direction of more-natural digestive health.

If you are reading this, chances are, you have eaten a standard modern diet, have possibly consumed antibiotics (which have affected your microbiome), and likely have not consumed a very divine diet. As you begin your journey into healing in this regard, you may want to consider a healthcare-provider-supervised period of gut rest, juice-feasting, and/or fasting. Often, we need the opportunity to reset our guts in order to begin to heal. Adding things like chia, aloe, flax, coconut meat, and Vitamix-level blending (see Chapter 2) are particularly helpful for this healing phase.

An additional critical component to proper digestion is chewing. We do not chew our food the way we would have if we were out in nature. Digestion actually begins in the mouth with saliva, enzymatic reactions, and the chewing process. Technically speaking, you should chew every bite until your tongue cannot identify what the things in your mouth were when you first placed them there. Experts estimate each bite should be chewed 50-100 times. This both aids in the digestive process by breaking it down in your mouth and allows time for the enzymes to work.

One more time, bringing this back to The Secret of Life, although the convenience of modern society has allowed us the opportunity to have 24-hour access to food, the reality is – we are not designed to consume food late in the evening. Our ancestors would not have been eating in the middle of the night – and we should not either. As best you can, within the dictates of your life's schedule, ideally, you should not eat past 8:30pm. This time also gives your gut a break and a chance to rest and heal.

CHAPTER 6

Stress

"Stress is unavoidable and often out of our control.
How we adapt to it and overcome it is not."
-Doc Love

There's mental stress and there's physiological stress. Sometimes, the first causes the second. Sometimes, physiological stress is present – even when our mind is good and happy. The stress response is running anytime the physiological stress mechanism is activated in the body. As we discussed previously, the physiological stress response involves a cascade of hormones and biochemical processes that occur whether you are conscious of them or not.

When the stress hormone response fires, your body receives doses of cortisol, epinephrine, and norepinephrine, your adrenals fire, and your blood chemistry changes. The stress response affects your blood pressure and cholesterol-production levels. It downgrades insulin-receptors, resulting in more glucose (sugar) in the blood. It lowers sex-hormone-binding-globulin, which allows for more free sex-hormones in the bloodstream, which are very mitogenic and can become cancerous if not well-regulated. Many people with weight problems, emotional problems, and energy problems may likely be suffering from Sympathetic Overload Syndrome and/or adrenal fatigue as a result of a prolonged period of chronic fight-or-flight stress-that they may not have been consciously aware of. For example, our bodies are exposed to extraordinary amounts of radiation, electromagnetic fields, microwaves, and cellular waves, and Wi-Fi each and every day. This exposure can cause an inflammatory physiological response in the body, putting some people in Fight-or-Flight, which may cause blood sugar regulation, weight, or other problems without ever being consciously aware of where it came from.

Mental, emotional, spiritual, or psychological stress can also wreak havoc on the mind and body. There are a myriad of techniques available, in addition to traditional psychological counseling, to take control of these stresses and your reaction to them. We will discuss many of these techniques in Chapter 13: The Divine Mind. However, it is of the upmost importance that we note at this point that health, including mental, emotional, spiritual, and psychological health, is a total sum game. Everything that we have addressed up to this point in this book, along with many of the things that we have yet to discuss, play into your potential ability to adapt, heal, and overcome these stressors. What you eat, how well you digest and assimilate it, your level of hydration, and your nervous system's ability to send and receive signals and adapt efficiently all factor into how well you can or cannot handle mental stress.

CHAPTER 7

Movement

"Motion is life.
The opposite of motion is rigor mortis, death."
-Doc Love

If I could give you a magic pill that would prevent 62% of Alzheimer's Disease, 50% of all stroke deaths, 63% of Congestive Heart-Disease deaths, 60% of all breast cancer, 72% of lung cancer in smokers, 72% of melanoma cases, 50% of colon cancers, 50% of all cases of heart disease, normalize blood pressure, cholesterol and triglyceride levels, increase strength, flexibility, and balance, enhance learning capacity by up to 12x, increase serotonin and dopamine levels, and increase immune system function, would you take it? Of course you would! Here is your prescription: the magic pill is a 30-minute walk every day. A simple, brisk, 30-minute walk can radically change your health factors in nearly every category.

So again, here you are, placed on this earth, no cities, no cars, no roads – how do you get around? You walk. If you can make friends with a horse or an elephant – cool, but otherwise, you walk around everywhere you go. Your genetic code expects you to be moving about this earth a certain amount every single day. Your tissues, your organs, your blood flow, your lymph flow – have all come to depend on that movement in order to maintain your overall health. Your natural environment would not have concrete floors and blacktop. Your natural design does not include modern shoes (we will discuss shoes more in the next chapter), furniture, or cars. In a tribal existence, you would squat more often, pick things up more often, and likely lift, pull, and climb more often in the natural course of the day. We certainly would not spend hours of our life in a chair, or a car, or staring at a computer screen. I am sure that you've seen the meme by now, and it's true: sitting is this generation's smoking. The effects of our stagnant lifestyle on our health will be measured across our generation over the next couple of decades, but the early numbers are not good. In cases of degeneration and spinal decay, sitting is to the spine like sugar is to the teeth (i.e. cavities).

Knowing that you're designed to move, your exercise should be a reflection of this and involve whole-body movement. Infants and animals provide an excellent example of what our natural movement profiles should look like. Upon waking: an immediate whole-body stretch! Followed immediately by tuning in to any isolated areas that need to be stretched. Just like an infant, cross-crawl movements stimulate brain function and brain health. Movement is literally a nutrient for your brain and body.

Appropriate exercise should stimulate our body and never hurt. If you cause yourself pain, you have done too much and have gone too far. Appropriate exercise will increase focus, energy, blood and oxygen flow, cerebrospinal fluid flow, and help regulate insulin receptors. Much attention should be paid to heart rate and intensity zones and understanding the goals and outcomes of your exercise.

Flexibility is a key component of a healthy, muscular, ligamentous, fascial system. Using appropriate stretching techniques, as well as any variety of massage, can increase the pliability, resilience, and flexibility of your body. We regularly receive reflexology, massage, and a combination of passive and active stretching as a part of our total health regimen.

A naturally congruent exercise and movement routine, along with a Divine diet, will help your body approach its Source-given set-weight, whatever that weight may be for you.

CHAPTER 8

Breathing

"It's the first thing you do, and the last thing you do.
There's probably something to it in between."
-Doc Love

Breathing is likely the most unconscious thing that you do day-in and day-out your entire life. Thankfully, we don't have to consciously think about breathing – our innate design just does it for us. BUT, what if we do think about it?

Breathing and breathwork is the #1, easiest way to bio-hack your physiology. Observations from yogis and scientists across the ages have shown us that there is a breath for every physiological state. Simple examples: You breathe differently when you walk versus powerwalk versus jog versus sprint. You breathe differently when you sleep versus in your common, waking day. You breathe differently when you are angry with someone than when you are laughing. There is a breath for when you are suddenly startled, a breath for a horrific scream, a breath for a joyous surprise, and a different breath for an orgasm!

Recognizing these observations and states to be true, it stands to reason that you can reverse engineer your physiology using your breath just as easily as your physiology creates specific breaths for specific states. In fact, whole fields of study and practice are built upon this premise. There are many forms of breathwork and breathwork practitioners around the world. The more you master your ability to breathe, the more you will master your physiology and your state management. Even the United States Navy Seals study and practice breathwork as part of their regimen.

Breathing can calm or excite the body. While breathing directly affects oxygen saturation, different breaths also elicit different hormone cascades in the brain and body. There are breaths for relaxing and breaths for powering up. Each of these will cause a different physiological cascade.

Daily practices can have a dramatic effect on your health and wellbeing. Do you think your life would be better or worse with more or less oxygen? Can you consciously breathe differently every day for a minute or two and have a dramatic effect on your lifetime level of oxygen? Of course you can. How different do you think your cellular makeup will be in two years if you consistently oxygenate? Can you make sessions in a hyperbaric oxygen chamber a regular part of your life and wellness routine? Studies have shown remarkable changes in the health of those who use hyperbaric oxygen chambers regularly.

If you want to become a master of your breath and altering your physiological state at any given time, you will want to study one or more of the different breathing arts. We regularly practice Tony Robbins' Priming exercise. We also regularly practice Somato-Respiratory Integration (SRI). Based on <u>The Twelve Stages of Healing</u>, SRI teaches the breaths, postures, motions, and declarations associated with each stage of healing. Having command over these processes allows you to appropriately process any stage of healing that you are currently in, and to have access to any other stage that you want to be in.

These exercises not only oxygenate your body, but also activate the various physiological states and their resultant hormone cascades of each stage of healing. Activating your physiology on purpose is a powerful way to take control of your state and your healing.

CHAPTER 9

Funny Shoes

"You have brains in your head. You have feet
in your shoes. You can steer yourself in any
direction you choose." – Dr. Seuss

Modern society has not been designed with our natural design and/or movement in mind. Concrete and blacktop, while great for sidewalks, parking lots, and buildings, does not, in any way, mimic the natural walking surfaces that we would encounter in an average day walking this earth with no cities, no cars, and no roads. And-while fashionable and convenient, almost all modern footwear has a detrimental effect on our natural, rhythmic movement and gait patterns. The following information will not win you any fashion points and will likely not be popular amongst most of you. It will, however, change some of your lives, cure some of your ails, and restore any of you who try it (and stick with it) to a more natural, divine pattern of movement.

A number of years back, a rather brilliant Swiss engineer came to study the Masai tribes of Africa. What he found in this tribe of people, who have walked barefoot since the dawn of time, and often traveled miles upon miles each day barefoot, is that their culture does not even have words for "foot pain", "ankle pain", "knee pain", or "low back pain". With agreement from the elders, he studied them – how they walked, and what was different about their gait and postural patterns compared to most industrialized society.

What he found was remarkably simple – yet profound. How we walk as humans, barefoot, on semi-soft and uneven ground, is radically different from how we walk in modern shoes, on concrete, and engages a completely different set of postural muscles through the whole kinetic chain – literally from toe to head.

Almost all modern shoes include a 5-7mm drop from heel to toe and have a rigid bottom, causing a klop-klop effect from heel-strike to toe-land as we walk. This engages a certain set of postural muscles and encourages a forward posture of the head to keep the balance of your body centered as you imitatively fall forward each step. It encourages longer strides and a more aggressive forward-leaning posture. Our natural, Source-given, barefoot walking pattern involves a soft heel-strike, a rolling foot, and a small, ball-of-the-foot-divot in the ground, keeping the center of gravity directly upright and activating a completely different, normalized set of postural muscles. This is how we are designed to walk on this earth. He set about to design shoes which mimic this pattern. His first result was the MBT. His most recent is kyBoot. Both of these brands mimic your natural, Source-given walking pattern and will change the biomechanics of your every step. When you first start with either of them, you will need to gradually work your way into wearing them, but then continue to wear them for 90 days straight to change your neuromuscular walking pattern.

Taking this whole concept a step further, you have toes! Look down and see them – lift your foot if you have to, but they are there. They are NOT an accident. In modern society, our toes have been relegated to after-thoughts crammed into the front of overtight shoes. In your design, however, your toes are an important and vital part of your movement and well-being. Vibram's Five-Fingers are shoes designed with your toes in mind. They are incredible and a great way for you to have a barefoot walking experience with a minimalist-protective foot covering. Now, that being said, they – and you – are not designed to walk on concrete. They are amazing, but you should use them in natural environments. Relatedly, any chance that you have to be barefoot in safe, natural environments, should be taken. In addition to grounding and electron-transfer, there is a whole science to reflexology through the points on the feet. You were designed with this in mind. After all, if you were put on this earth with no cities, no cars, no roads, you would never have known anything different.

CHAPTER 10

Posture

"Don't slouch."-Mary Poppins

Even the most ancient cultures understood that a balanced, upright posture, was a strong indicator of a vibrant, healthy life, while a slumped, hunched over posture, was a strong indicator of weakness, frailty, sickness, and mortality. Modern studies correlate this today. There is a direct relationship between your measurable posture and range of motion and your mortality.

Try this exercise for me: Imagine, picture in your mind, a sad, depressed person. What do they look like? Are they slumped? Are they hunched over? Are they curled in? How did you know? It's because every physiological state has an associated posture and every posture has an associated physiological state.

Our modern lifestyle has changed so dramatically in the last 100 years, and exponentially so in the last 25 years. One hundred years ago (and before that throughout the course of history), people still did regular, manual labor in their daily life. Think about how much you would move and work every day on this Earth – no cities, no cars, no roads. Most people had animals of one form or another to care for, grew gardens, and walked, carrying what they needed most everywhere that they went. Jobs were almost all labor-related and the result was a slimmer, fitter, more agile population of people. The second half of the last century saw a shift towards more dependence on cars, convenience, and desk-based jobs. The incredible, rapid evolution of technology, ushering us into the information age of the last 25 years, has shifted our entire species profile into a much more sedentary, docile existence.

Technology has afforded us great advantages but has also dramatically changed the way that we live. We have machines and services that do most all of our labor activities for us. The shift from labor to information has caused a species meant to move 8-10 hours a day to now sit 8-10 hours a day. Just think about an average day: sit in your car (or a bus) to get to where you're going, sit at your desk for the majority of the day, sit in transportation on your way home, to come home and sit in your living room until you go to bed, to do it all over again the next day. Maybe you'll get out on the weekend, but the majority of your days and life will be spent sedentary. Sit, sit, sit. And – as we have already said, sitting is the new smoking. This shift in our daily life, paired with the advent of drive-through fast food and all the agricultural shifts we spoke about in Chapter 2, has ushered in an epidemic of obesity in the United States from the 1980's to the present.

Your posture affects your energy. Your posture, plus your range of motion, affects your agility and your nervous system's ability to receive and process information. Nearly everything in our modern life affects our posture, and unfortunately, mostly in a negative way. Screens, from computers to smartphones, encourage Anterior Head Carriage, or Forward Head Posture. Our shoes encourage a Forward Body Posture. Driving, and even most motorcycle set-ups encourage bad posture. Most desk chairs and couches are not ergonomically designed either.

While there are good beds available, most mattresses do not truly support your spinal posture when you sleep. Bed technology is ever-evolving, but for now, we recommend Sleep Number or Tempurpedic. If you're going with a Tempurpedic, we recommend trying an entire line, finding the one that you feel the most comfortable on, and actually purchasing the one that is one-level firmer than that one. Additionally, you should pay special attention to the pillow that you choose to sleep on. You spend 6-8 hours per night sleeping in a certain position, which teaches your cervical spine (neck) how to exist in a certain posture. You should choose a pillow that encourages proper spinal position while you sleep. Great examples include the Tempurpedic Neck Pillow and the Therapeutica Pillow.

So, it's up to you. You are going to have to become conscious about your posture, your environment, and your choices. For starters, you are going to have to choose products that support you in your postural journey. Ergonomic chairs, lumbar supports in your car, perhaps even choosing a giant inflatable exercise ball in place of an office chair. When you're on your phone, it should be held at the level of your eyes instead of tucking your head to look down, which can cause "text neck". If you have children, or if you still carry a backpack regularly, you should investigate things like the "Back-T-Pack", a true, physiologically-designed postural support backpack, as opposed to most backpacks, which encourage you to lean forward to counter the weight you are carrying. Does your work environment allow for the possibility of a standing desk? Or a convertible sit-to-stand desk?

Beyond being conscious about your posture, your environment, and your choices, you are likely going to need to do some self-corrective work to restore yourself from years of bad postural habits and related muscle imbalances, in order to return to your Source-given, postural design. The simplest program that you can do daily (or multiple times per day) – for free – is the Straighten Up America program of spinal hygiene exercises, which can easily be done in any environment in just a few minutes. They are a great way to start your day and an easy add-in throughout the day to encourage your body towards a more Source-given, postural design.

For a more advanced postural re-education, you are going to want to engage with experts in modalities like stretching and yoga. Our highest recommendation goes to those who have been trained in Egoscue. There are Egoscue centers around the country and the world designed specifically to help you rebalance your postural muscles so that you can pursue other activities like yoga and stretching with appropriate posture, without further reinforcing bad habits and patterns.

One more exercise: We have found that many people have been taught a very limited posture when it comes to prayer. While there is no wrong way to pray, we would like to afford you the opportunity to try a different posture and see if it affects your connection to Source. In a private space, extend your arms out to the sides, pull your shoulders back, open your chest and heart, keep your palms up, head back, face up, turning your gaze to the heavens. With your heart wide open, have a conversation with Source.

If this posture allows you to be more open, more reverent, more loving, then please, use it freely.

CHAPTER 11

Sleep

"You will spend 25-33% of your entire life sleeping."

-Doc Love

Sleep is one of the most important elements of overall health. It is when much of your body's healing and growth occur. For your overall health, you want your sleep to be on a recurring, timely schedule, which your body can learn to count on and build natural rhythms with. Think about it this way, if you were placed on this earth, no cities, no cars, no roads – When would you go to sleep? When the sun goes down. When would you wake up? When the sun comes up. Ideally, your sleep coincides with nighttime and waking coincides with the sun coming up. We understand that this may not be a possibility for all immediately, but long term, it should be a priority for your health.

Your body needs regularity so that it can develop rhythms and cycles for healing and growth that it can count on. Your body needs to know that it has a safe, regular, repeating ability to go through NREM and REM sleep. REM (rapid eye movements) sleep is where healing and growth occur. Both the amount and the quality of your sleep must be sufficient. In addition, the time that you actually go to sleep makes a difference. Studies suggest that every hour of sleep prior to midnight is equal to two hours of sleep after midnight. There is a distinct and measurable health difference between those who go to bed at 10pm and get up at 6am, and those who go to bed at 1am and get up at 9am, even though they both got eight hours of sleep.

While you should do your best to have no stress 30 minutes prior to bed, no blue-light exposure, no food or drink, and no workout, nothing is more important to your sleep than the environment that you sleep in. Your sleep environment should be dark and quiet. When we say dark, we mean *completely*. Sleep studies have shown that the little light in the corner of the television (when it is off) or the illumination of the electric alarm clock are both prominent disruptors of REM sleep. Your sleep environment should be completely dark. Duct tape (or electrical tape) can cover small lights (like the tv). Blackout curtains can cover windows from letting in light from the outside. You may just have to get a new alarm clock – one that does not light up. There should be no electricity or electrical field active within 6 feet of your bed. Having your phone plugged in on the nightstand is a sure-fire way to have interrupted sleep. Move it (and anything like it) 6 feet or more away from your bed.

Relatedly, if you are going to be on your phone, tablet, laptop, or watch TV 30 minutes before bed, you should wear blue-light filtering glasses. In addition, if it is reasonable to do it in your home, you should put your WiFi on a timer to shut down while you sleep. We are all bombarded with enough signal every day, one less source at night is a positive step for your health.

In an ideal world, you should think of your sleeping environment as a sanctuary. It would not be a place that you work, eat, stress, or watch television. It is meant for peace, relaxation, rest, and sleep. You should sleep on your back, on a firm mattress, with a proper pillow. You should choose a pillow that encourages proper spinal posture while you sleep. Great examples include the Tempurpedic Neck Pillow and the Therapeutica Pillow.

There is no such thing as "catching up" on sleep. There is some limited research which suggests that you may be able to sleep ahead, or get extra sleep for an anticipated lack, but once you have missed it, it is gone. You cannot trade hours today for hours tomorrow. Sleep has become a non-negotiable issue at every example of high performance, even the United States Navy Seals have a mandatory sleep schedule to keep them at their best.

Sleep is when many new cells are made. When we think about your total cellular turnover, sleep is an essential piece of that equation. Taking steps to improve your sleep is taking steps to improve your cellular turnover. The current state of your cells is the product of the last couple of years of sleep that you have had. Imagine what your cellular makeup could look like in two years with better healing through better sleeping habits!

CHAPTER 12

Sunlight & Dirt

"You are basically a house plant with overcomplicated feelings."
-adapted from Reza Farazmand

We already know that you need water. Turns out, you need sunlight and dirt too – or, at least, your Source-given design expects it. If you were put here on this earth, no cities, no cars, no roads, you would spend a lot of time in the dirt and under the sun. As we discussed in previous chapters, the nutrients and healthy cofactors that come from these processes are essential for your overall well-being. You need Vitamin D in sufficient levels, which you can make from exposure to the sun – if you are in the right sun and have all of the necessary cofactors. For starters, most of us are not in the right sun. You need to be within 18 degrees of the equator, in the peak of the day, with approximately 80% of your body exposed in order to get the correct ratio of UV-A to UV-B rays to produce a sufficient amount of Vitamin D. For most of us, this is not the case. If you want a quick look into the difference these ratios of rays can make, think about the colors of the flora, fauna, and animals of the Caribbean versus those of upstate New York. There is an entire world of vibrance and color that is possible near the equator, that is no longer possible the further away you get from it. If you were to spend time during the peak of the sun in upstate New York, you would be receiving different amounts of UV-A vs UV-B rays, which may actually be detrimental to your health. But even in upstate New York, some sun exposure can be good for you. Since we're talking about sun exposure, this is a great time to mention that most sunscreen is highly toxic and very dangerous for both you and the environment.

Because it is difficult to create sufficiency in Vitamin D levels in today's modern society based on sunlight exposure alone, it is essential to supplement with it. Be sure to choose a high quality, Vitamin D3 supplement to achieve this goal.

We spoke earlier in the book about the importance of the dirt that your food is grown in and how the healthy bacteria in the dirt affect your microbiome. This is why eating locally and organic is such a great option; it's dirt from your environment, and therefore bacteria from your environment, that you interact with every day. We are meant to interact with our environment and our dirt. Our kids should be given every opportunity to play in natural dirt to help build their immune systems and help them connect to earth. With this in mind, although the local "Yard of the Month" award is a nice prize, we should be cautious and aware of any toxins, poisons, and/ or feed that we are spraying on our yards and around our homes, where our kids and/or animals may be playing, or where it may get into our air system.

There are numerous studies exploring and supporting the benefits of grounding, which involves time spent connecting "skin to dirt" (or grass). If we were placed on this earth, no cities, no cars, no roads, we would definitely find ourselves connected to earth often – if not at all times. Find a way to create this opportunity in your life on a regular and recurring basis to see what opportunities it holds for you.

CHAPTER 13

Divine Mind

"Thoughts become things."-Old Proverb

Of all of the tools that can work for or against us in our health journey, none are so powerful as the mind. Where attention goes, energy flows. We know from science that the placebo effect is not only real, but that it is arguably more powerful than any real effect we can have in any given clinical, scientific situation through therapeutics, surgeries or drugs. The power of the human mind to shape, change, and create our reality, including our health, is unlimited.

That being said, at this point in modern society, we can no longer control all of the thoughts being introduced to our minds. Everything in our environment has an effect on what we think. They say that we become the average of the five people that we spend the most time around; the reason for this is that we affect each other and entrain to our surroundings, belief systems, energies, and behaviors. Conforming to be like our tribe is in our human nature.

Unfortunately, in the information age, we are bombarded with input on a daily basis that we did not ask for, may not want, and may not even realize that we are receiving. Think about what inputs you would have received if you were just put on this Earth – no cities, no cars, no roads. Colorful berries and foods in the wild would have been the one of the most exciting stimuli to regularly stimulate our brains. Today, the field of psychological marketing literally plays on our subconscious to entice us to buy things or participate in certain segments of society. The colors of apps on your smartphone are designed to mimic the colors of berries and foods in the wild in order to stimulate and excite your brain each time you see them. The same is true of the candy bars you get bombarded with when you find yourself trapped in the checkout aisle at the local grocery store, candy surrounding you in all the colors, on both sides. Your brain sees the colors and gets excited that you have just found nutrient dense food stores for your body in the wilderness. In reality, you have most certainly not. Every day, we are confronted with advertisements in internet videos, television, radio, and even print, from magazines to billboards, that we cannot avoid. The best that we can do is attempt to control as much of our home and work environment as we can to limit external influence that we do not want and fill our lives with influences that we *do* want.

There are a nearly infinite number of techniques and methods to train your mind. You should try many of them and master each one that resonates and works with you. Some foundational pillars to give yourself the best chance at maintaining a Source-connected mindset, begin with creating the supportive circumstances in the other parts of your life that we've discussed in this book: food, movement, nervous system health, sleep, etc. Then, with routine and regularity, you can begin to apply all of the mental, emotional and spiritual techniques available. We recommend that you study as many of the ancient wisdom traditions as you are able to expose yourself to and take from them each piece that works.

The simplest example that we can think of is the practice of meditation. Meditation has probably been around as long as humans have been around. There are nearly an infinite variety of techniques available to help you meditate. What we know through modern science is that the most effective techniques, when practiced regularly and repetitively, alter your brain waves and thus, your physiological state. In your average, normal awake state, your brain operates in Beta. Through focused meditation, you can achieve states of Alpha, Theta, and even Delta, although Delta is most commonly associated only with deep sleep. When considering different meditative techniques, you should research to see if any studies have been conducted to show that technique's influence on brain wave state.

There are multiple devices which can be used to also help you achieve these states. One such device, which we love and use, is the NuCalm. NuCalm's technology and process has been studied and shown to consistently aid the brain and body in achieving Alpha and Theta states. It is a multi-faceted approach, which is highly effective in today's modern world.

Some examples of techniques, programs, and teachers that have worked well for us include the Law of Attraction, the teachings of Abraham Hicks, A Course in Miracles, the writings of Rumi, Wayne Dyer, Brene Brown, John DeMartini, Candace Pert, Joe Dispenza, Tony Robbins, Marianne Williamson, Donny Epstein, the Tao Te Ching, The Bible, the Metaphysical Bible, the Gnostic Gospels, and the ancient wisdom teachings of the Masons.

In addition to the above, we have used other techniques as well. Pets have been shown to have an amazing effect on our mindset and wellbeing. Daily affirmations and gratitude are also beneficial to our state of mind. In our office, at our morning huddle before we begin the day, and the evening debrief as we end each day, we share our gratitudes as a team. We strongly control our environment as best we can, to include positive and funny memes on our computers, to happy music playing over our speakers. Our team even created a Spotify playlist called "Every Happy Song Ever (Clean)".

One particularly helpful tool that we developed years ago (and use every day) is called "The Identity Card". Take a 3x5 notecard and begin to write (vertically) "I am" statements of all of the identities that you currently hold as positive in your life and/or wish to hold. You can also add "I have" statements to differentiate roles you used to have from those you wish to own and be known as now. You may have been "Mary's Son" or "Fred's Little Girl" before, and you may wish to change those identities and roles in your life now. It doesn't change your relation or love, necessarily, but it can change your identity and how you are seen. For example, if you walked into a restaurant in your home town, would you rather have folks say, "There's Mary's son!" or "Hey, there's Jim, his Mom's Mary!" There are appropriate ages and times for every identity. But there are also times to set new identity standards for yourself and affirm them and walk in them everyday.

An example:

I am (name you prefer to be known as).
I am a (Doctor), (who facilitates healing).
I am a (Minister).
I am a (Chef), (who cooks for my family & friends).
I am a (Lover).
I am (Enthusiastic/Intelligent).
I am (Fit/Healthy).

I have a (Mom/Dad), her name is (Name).
I have a (Brother/Sister), his name is (Name).
I attend school at (School Name).
I work at (Job).

Take this card out every morning as soon as you wake up and read it out loud to yourself, preferably in the mirror. This simple process of anchoring your identities in your own words, in your own writing, in your own voice, before the world begins to project things at you will help you become and achieve who and what you want with faster results and greater clarity. It is one of the most powerful exercises that we know of. And one of the best parts of it is-you can do it again as needed! The card you make today does not have to be your forever card. These cards should probably be reviewed at least annually in your life to see if they are serving your highest good!

Another of the most powerful forces known to man is laughter. If you have ever heard one of a baby's first giggles and felt the sensation of joy ripple through your being, then you know what we are talking about. If you have ever been watching a movie and laughed until the point of physical pain, then you know what we are talking about. If you have ever been yelling at someone – so angrily – until you said something stupid by mistake and instantly laughed, interrupting your anger, and then found it difficult to go back to the argument, then you know what we are talking about. Laughing and laughter are a Source-given tool for goodness. You do not have to even hear anything funny to start laughing. You can start laughing at any time, for no reason at all, and keep laughing until it's funny. Around the world, and maybe in your area, there are laughing meditation groups. With the technology of the world at our fingertips, we have never had more access to instantly watch or hear something funny, which can change our entire day, as we do now. There is never an excuse for not finding something positive or happy in the world.

We would be negligent not to mention the absolute healing and freeing power of Forgiveness. Nearly all of the influential people we mentioned a few paragraphs ago emphasize forgiveness in their work. Forgiveness is not always straight forward or easy, but it is an incredible healing tool at your disposal, when you are ready. It is said that forgiveness doesn't make what happened to you ok, it just makes you ok. And forgiving ourselves may sometimes be our biggest hurdle. Please be kind to yourself. Show yourself Grace. You are worthy.

Bringing it full circle, back to Law of Attraction and Manifestation-thoughts become things. Where attention goes, energy flows. Where you put your focus matters. All things began as a thought in someone's mind. What now stands as the tallest building in the world – an incredible structure – a feat of ingenuity and engineering, began with a simple idea in one man's mind that he wanted to build the tallest building in the world. He believed it was possible and that he could do it. He then began to see what that building may look like, what all of the parts and pieces were, then began to think about the design. He knew it would happen. Then slowly, but surely, with attention and action, he shared his vision, enrolled others to believe and take action too, and what began as a thought has become the tallest structure on earth.

All of us may not be ready to jump right into building the next tallest building in the world, but all of us can begin to shape our thoughts, attentions, and actions purposefully into the direction of what will make us feel good, contribute, and generate happiness. Start where you are, and one day at a time, move in the direction that you want to be, knowing all the while that in the future, it's already done; you are just here experiencing the journey in your future's past. There are an infinite number of potential futures. Choose the one that you wish to live out.

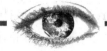

CHAPTER 14

Biofield & Energetics

"You are a latticework of energies."-Donna Eden

Though, in science, we are still only beginning to understand the biofield, its prevalence, influence, and importance cannot be understated. Mainstream, Quantum, and Noetic sciences are all studying the biofield individually, collectively, and through the lens of the Field to further our understanding of its role, influence, and importance.

What we know for sure is that we each possess a physical part and a non-physical part. A body and a spirit/soul/ energy. We also know that within our physicality, there are invisible fields of frequency, coherence, and interaction that simultaneously project information from us and receive information from others and/or the Field.

Take, for instance, our ECG/EKG heart signature. We can measure the heart and its projected energy field and signature up to 12 feet away. You can witness changes in the heart field of 2 or more people when they come within 12 feet of each other. Similar studies and observations are true of sEMG activity in bodily and muscular movement and EEG in brain waves. These are invisible forces related to our physical part which have a physically visible effect. Recent quantum, neurological, and energetic sciences suggest that there are other invisible organizing fields of intelligence relating to and acting upon and with the body. Modern science has all but accepted that the mind is not housed within the brain, but rather, our most recent theories seem to indicate that the mind is a Field, and the brain acts more as an antenna interrelating to this organizing energy.

Regardless of the specifics of what we do and do not know, it is evident that invisible forces play a prominent role in our lives and physical wellbeing. We are subjected to more radiation, microwaves, EMF, and WiFi bombardment every single day than our ancestors would have been exposed to in their entire lifetime. Think about how much exposure we would have had if we were on this Earth – no cities, no cars, no roads, no computers, no cell phones, no internet, no TV. It does not appear that our exposure is going to lessen anytime soon; in fact, it would seem that it is only going to continually increase. With this in mind, we recommend using every responsibly-studied technology available to combat potentially detrimental invisible forces, while simultaneously connecting to and enhancing every invisible force which may benefit our health.

First and foremost, we need to use any available means of protecting ourselves against all of the pass-through waves that technology is putting through our bodies on a daily basis.

As of the publication of this book, the best way that we know now is called Q-Link SRT-3 technology. They offer a variety of products for your personal body, home, and technology, to dampen these interferences. Similar technology exists for cell phones in WaveShield and R2L Radiation-to-Light devices. Beyond technological help, we also need to exercise consciousness in how we use technology. Using speakerphone to keep devices away from our body is a healthy choice. Using speakerphone and setting it on your stomach is not a healthy choice. The same is true for laptops and/or tablets. Keeping them away from our bodies lessens the amount of exposure that we absorb.

There are numerous other biofield technologies which should be explored, including, but limited to: the BioCharger, the Bemer, Rife Technologies, the Magnesphere, PEMF Machines, BioMats, Orgonite, crystals and grounding blankets.

In addition to all of the technologies mentioned above, Energy-Healing is an ancient practice only beginning to be studied and understood by more modern science. Every year, new studies demonstrate the powerful effects various energy-healing techniques have on the body and wellbeing. While there are too many to go through in this book, we will say that we have had powerful personal experiences with receiving Reiki. When choosing a practitioner, it is important to know what level of training and commitment he or she has given to their art. Finding a Reiki Master who has pursued years of study and self-work, not just taken a weekend course, is a wise research decision. The same can be said for Acupuncture. There are weekend-course practitioners and those who have given 12+ years pursuing a doctorate in Chinese Medicine. Both of these techniques represent powerful healing modalities that can be of great benefit to your health and wellness journey.

Other lesser-known methods available for your exploration include EFT/Tapping, PSYCH-K, and the Oneness Blessing. Each of these have also had a powerful effect on our lives and we would be remiss if we did not mention them to you.

One additional area of great interest and recent scientific exploration is the study of Cymatics and Sound Healing. Much is yet to be understood about how deeply sound and frequency can affect and effect our physical and non-physical; but what is certain is that it can create powerful change. The study of frequency and vibration (and its visual representation) hold untold treasures for us. From the work of Dr. Masaru Emoto, showing us the visual change in water crystals through intention and sound, to the new emerging science of Cymatics, we look excitedly at the possibilities that lie ahead for healing in these fields and encourage their responsible exploration. Certainly, from ancient times to now: sounds, song, drumming, chanting and the like, have always had a place in healing culture around the world. From sound bowls and crystals to tuning forks and the nervous system, we still have much to learn and gain.

CHAPTER 15

Community, Tribe, Village

"It takes a village."-Old Proverb

We are tribal creatures. It's our natural state. We are meant to be in a tribe, a community, a village, a herd. We are meant to know our roles, know that we are needed, know that we contribute, know that we need others, and have appropriate social interactions within the context of our circle. Think about being placed on this Earth – no cities, no cars, no roads: How important is your community? Very likely, the level of cohesiveness with which you function as a team will have a direct correlation to how well your entire community survives and/or thrives.

Our modern world has made tribal existence confusing. We simultaneously have more and better access and communication than ever before in the history of man, and yet, many more of us feel more isolated and alone than ever before in the history of man either. Facebook and other social giants have thrived by connecting community in communication. Incredible success, the largest number of human interactions ever. Connecting the entire planet in a way never before seen. And yet, many of us struggle to connect. Struggle to know our place. Struggle to know if we contribute in any meaningful way, or if we can really count on anyone. Many of us have thousands of Facebook friends but cannot name our neighbors.

Many life lessons, indeed, ages of human wisdom are being lost in the shuffle of modern life and technology. Many of the social cues and life lessons once passed on through generations of men and women beside campfires and out on hunting parties are no longer being transmitted. Many cultural norms are long discarded. Birth and Death, once a revered and reverent part of the cycle of life in a tribal culture are often shielded and veiled in modern society. Our elder wisdom is not being passed down to new generations.

We must find the means to reclaim our communities and identities through this technological age. We must commit to deepening our resolve to connect with one another in true human interaction. The technology is not going anywhere. It will only evolve. But we must commit to evolving ourselves alongside it. There is an art to communication that is lost in technology. There is a biofield interaction that occurs when you are face to face or in a room together with other real people. Body language. Pheromones. Hormones. Field interactions. These are important components of our development, mentally, physically, emotionally, and spiritually.

We must find ways to turn old roles into new roles that fit with our changing technological and cultural environment.

And we must not forget that our code and our deep human needs do not change with the pace of our modern world.

There is a saying: "You become the average of the five people you spend the most time around". Never before have we had such an ability to create our own tribe and connect with a selection of exactly who we want to connect with. Technology makes it possible for us to control many of our interactions. To carve for ourselves space and intention to be in community with the people who we want and who will move us in the direction we want to go.

When Twitter came out and got popular, we made for ourselves a Twitter account that we thought of as our Twitter Board of Advisors. We only subscribed to follow the five people we most wanted influencing our lives at the time. Every day, our feed filled us with their influence and wisdom. We do the same with Facebook and who we see first in our feed (and who we block). Controlling your inputs and outputs will continue to be ever important in the evolving social technological future. Knowing that you contribute in a meaningful way, as well as receive, is necessary. This balance is commonly known as the Law of Giving and Receiving. There should be balance in all energy exchange in the universe. As you give, so you receive.

People behave according to the expectations of their peer group (and/or family). Make sure you set yourself up for success. Surround yourself with success-minded, health-minded, heart-minded, servant-hearted people and they will rub off on you by holding you to their level of service, love and expectations.

CHAPTER 16

Relationships

"I want a love like Johnny and June..."
-Heidi Newfield

Successful relationships begin long before you are in them. It starts with preparing yourself. Using principles that we have already discussed in this book, such as identity and law of attraction, your first job is to become the version of yourself that would attract and be worthy of your dream mate. Doing your self-work first and knowing your value assure that as you enter into a relationship with another, you do so on a solid foundation and with a focus on the relationship itself.

Once you have become the person that you need to be in order to be worthy of your dream mate, you must put yourself in the places where that person would be. Chances are, they are not just down the street. If they are, you are extremely fortunate. Once you have found each other, the work has just begun.

For starters, successful couples hang around other successful couples. Commit to telling one another the hard truth, but with love and compassion. Develop continually evolving communication skills. Explore your identities as divine masculine and sacred feminine. Engage common hobbies as well as individual hobbies. Be committed to opening your heart and mind and exploring spirituality together.

Do not take one another for granted. Almost everyone enters into marriage thinking that it is forever. And, if in premarital counseling, you were to ask most people what the one thing that would cause them to end their relationship in divorce would be, nearly all of them have an answer. What this shows, is that most couples actually enter into marriage believing in divorce. And, as it turns out, more than half of them end up that way. So, as you enter into a relationship, understand that in 5, 10, 20 years from now, you will be different people. Begin your journey together with the intention that you recognize this and grow and evolve together. Also commit to keeping a spark. Five years in, you should be able to still feel like it's your second date.

Since we are on the topic of relationships, let's talk about sex. Now, we know that sex doesn't only happen in relationships, but it is a great place to put it in this book. Sexual health and sacred sexuality are topics which are deserving of much more attention and conversation than they are currently being given in our modern society.

In a time when there has never been a greater exposure to sex and sexuality through porn and the internet, we are sadly lacking in conversations around its sacredness, fun, and safe practice.

Sex has been around since the beginning of time. The bottom line: it's how you got here, as well as everyone before you. From our grandparent's generation back, in the history of man, it was common for couples to marry and begin having children in their teenage years. That's because that's the age when sexual hormones kick in and for generations of humans, we knew that was normal. The tribe expected it and supported it. The elders guided and passed knowledge and wisdom. The middle-aged helped and taught lessons. It was a group effort.

Somewhere in the last century, it was decided that pregnancy, at any point before achieving your (or your parents') life goals for you, would ruin your life. This message has been driven into 2 generations of humans. In the course of trying to ensure our success, by keeping us "on track" and out of "trouble", the leaders in our society failed to recognize that the hormones did not change, and that all of that sacred knowledge needed to be passed down.

The push for abstinence and/or safe sex led to an incredible rise and dependence on hormone-based birth control. While scientifically effective at preventing pregnancy, we are only now beginning to see the long-term, epigenetic, and generational effects of these drugs. Rises in infertility, STD's, and reproductive irregularities are just some of the consequences that we are beginning to see at alarming levels in response to altering women's hormones for prolonged periods of time.

Sex is a natural, programmed process, part of our Source-given code. It comes with advantages and disadvantages, rewards and consequences. The hormones are going to kick in at the same age for every generation for the foreseeable future-roughly, their early teenage years. We must find ways to have meaningful conversations about responsible sex and sacred sexuality.

Within the context of relationships, communication is absolutely key, as you have likely both been raised in a culture where sex and sexuality has not been discussed openly. You both likely have misconceptions based on your fears, what you have experienced, and unrealistic expectations created by television, movies, and porn. Be open to each other's needs and desires, and explore together in a safe and conscious way.

CHAPTER 17

Pregnancy & Birth

"Nature does not hurry, yet everything
is accomplished."-Lao Tzu

So you're on this planet, no cities, no cars, no roads... and you find yourself pregnant! WOW! Congrats! Now what?

FIRSTLY-you need to know-this ^^^ has been the case for nearly every birth that has ever occurred in the history of humanity. Modern births, in all their numbers are a minor blip on the radar of how many humans have come into and through this world. Nearly all of them did not have hospitals, doctors, epidurals, etc. And YOU are the product of that lineage.

Now, a quick note: Emergency procedures are AMAZING! We love them, the doctors and nurses that perform them (total rockstars!), and we are glad to know they are there if you need them. Hygiene and sterilization, running water, and certain tools have all made birth an even safer and more successful event than it has been at certain points in history. BUT-we're going to talk about how you're made and how you're designed.

You (for the females reading) are MADE to give birth! It's amazing. Not all of you will. And that's ok too. But you are the only creatures on this planet who can create the next generation of human life! Pretty amazing! Men-did you read that? Amazing! You should look upon our female counterparts with the utmost respect just from that one point! Females are built with all the tools, parts and programming to incubate little humans! It's incredible!

Your body KNOWS what to do. The programming is already inside you! While we, the authors, are doctors- how arrogant and crazy to think any of us know more than the human body which is processing trillions upon trillions of perfect, ever-changing, ever complex reactions and processes at any given moment from the minute of conception to birth, and all the way through breastfeeding! Just an example-did you know that after birth, as breastfeeding progresses, that mom and baby's bodies still communicate and that the actual composition of the breastmilk changes according to the needs of the baby? What!?! Wow!

Everything about pregnancy and birth is a part of our Source-given design. And everything we've talked about so far in this book applies to birth as well. Nutrition, Movement, Nervous System Health, Biomechanics, Mindset-all matter! Not only for you in the process, but epigenetically what you're passing down as well!

There are SOOOO many options in birth. Please, please, please-explore your options (with your partner as it applies) and educate yourself. This is YOUR birth process. Whether in the hospital or not, you may want to learn about natural birth options, and you most certainly want to have a written-out birth plan.

What laboring positions do you want to utilize and explore during your labor and delivery? While some women deliver their babies while laboring on their backs, many women find that squatting or being on all-fours makes more physiological and gravitational sense! Some women prefer water births or shower births. Some want an orgasmic birth. Some prefer hypnobirthing. Some want all the options available.

Have a plan for when you want to cut the umbilical cord. Many experts agree that delayed cord-cutting is beneficial to the baby as he/she can receive more nutrients from the placenta, even after birth. Have a written plan for what happens immediately after birth (with no emergencies). Does the baby come directly to mom's chest? This promotes comfort through skin to skin contact. It also gives the baby comfort being near mom's heart-a sound that it has heard for months and months. If baby opens their eyes-their field of focus is only between 7 and 14 inches-precisely the range of distance from breast to face. Miraculous design! Will you instantly attempt a latch for breastfeeding? Should the baby be cleaned or do you want to leave the vernix coating on the skin for a while? Should the baby experience any shots or tests or can they be delayed? Personally, we feel that it's just not nice to smack a baby's butt first thing out of the womb, nor to prick and pierce its perfect Source-designed outer covering right away. Will your baby have its nervous system checked for interference right away?

Birth isn't always a super smooth and easy process. Should your baby have a chance to start with an interference-free nervous system? Talk with your birth team. Get agreement on what YOU feel is important. This is your Dream Birth. Design it as best you can ahead of time to be the way you want it.

In addition to hospitals, many people don't know that there are many birth options. Your area may be fortunate enough to have a birth center. Or perhaps you'd be most comfortable with a home birth. Are you aware of your options with a midwife? Going back to our tribal days, this was the standard model for thousands of years and billions of births. In many cases, all the women of a tribe or family participated in every birth in the community. Men and children were not separated and relegated to the waiting room. Birth was revered and seen as a miraculous part of our circle of life.

Every step in the birth process has a Source-given purpose. In a smooth, natural birth, did you know that Baby actually sends the signal for Mom to release oxytocin and begin labor? Baby tells you when it's ready! Due dates are our best guess at a generalized time frame. They should not be taken as final and absolute timelines. If you were put on this earth, no cities, no cars, no roads, would you even keep up with each day on a counting basis or would you connect and feel and participate in wonder as your birth progresses?

C-Sections are amazing and can save lives. However, they are commonly overused. It gives the doctor and hospital more control over what is happening and the timing of it, as it is a surgery and more of a predictable process. In an emergency, this is an incredible option. But short of an emergency, you should fully educate yourself by watching c-sections online in videos, reading about pros and cons and after-effects, and discuss with your birth team whether or not this is an appropriate option for you.

The natural birth process is Source-designed. First-Mom's body is designed to give birth. There is an entire progressing hormone cascade to allow each step to occur, and quite frankly, each of those steps is important for her safety, the baby's safety and for her healing and recovery after birth. Second-for Baby-each step has a purpose and meaning. As baby's head progresses through the birth canal, the pressure exerted upon its little cranial bones helps to shape the head and enhance cerebrospinal fluid flow. The baby gets exposure to natural immunoglobulins and micro bacteria as they progress through the canal, an important early step in immune development. The same happens with breastmilk. Literally every step has a purpose-so if you skip any steps, via choice or emergency, have some conversations with your team about what you can do to fulfill those purposes that get skipped.

The bottom line: birth is a natural and safe, amazing process! While our media and our mainstream medical system have turned it into something to fear or something to schedule, we want you to know that pregnancy and birth are a miracle and should be seen with awe and wonder.

CHAPTER 18

Immune System Development

"A cell cannot be in defense and growth at
the same time."-Bruce Lipton, PhD

As an immediate follow-up to birth, we must discuss immune system development. The topics that accompany immune development can be a hot button for some people.

Immunity and Immune System development are part of your Source-given design. There are very important timelines and progress steps to make sure your immune system develops according to its design. Much of our immune development depends on getting natural exposure to things through natural channels at appropriate times and levels.

As we have mentioned before in this book-letting your kids play in the dirt and having pets around enhance exposure and immune development! Maybe don't use anti-bacterial soap all the time, killing off all the bacteria that may potentially help your immune system. Natural birth and breastfeeding are both immune-building processes. Did you know that breastmilk contains immunoglobulins for baby that you cannot get from any other source?

But we can't complete this topic without at least briefly discussing vaccines and vaccine science. This is one of the hottest topics in the media at the time of publication of this book. People are very passionate about their stances. Emotions are raw. It becomes difficult to have good, science-based conversation because of all the emotions and fears surrounding the subject.

For starters, wouldn't you think that any conversation about vaccines should begin with all parties having a solid grasp on our natural immune development? We want to work WITH this process. When we try to do better than it, work faster than it, or beat it, we nearly always lose, scientifically speaking. All our conversations should focus on how to shape vaccines, vaccine science and vaccine scheduling to align with our natural immune development processes. Particular attention should be paid to TH1 and TH2 immune development pathways and timing, natural or oral exposure vs. injection into the bloodstream, as well as live vs. attenuated or synthetic strains.

Can conversations be had about germ theory and herd immunity-whether they can stand the test of science or have just been a theory and a talking point? About who is a disease carrier? Can you be fully vaccinated and carry and pass the things you have immunity to?

About whether these are our only options or if we can/ should educate our people and our corporations in a direction of more natural and congruent health? We must have conversations with scientists and authorities about our vaccine ingredients and processes. Are the adjuvants currently being used required, or are they the best that can be used? Mercury, thimerosal? Aluminum? Fetal cells? Can we do better?

Do we get a choice in our healthcare and belief systems and whether or not to participate? Is it all or nothing, or do we have room for choice and balance? If we do not participate, what must we commit ourselves to in order to protect ourselves, our families, and our communities? What immunity and health building responsibilities do we then bear?

Can we have a discussion involving the known harms around the current application of vaccines and the vaccine schedule? It's an established fact that there will be harm to a percentage of the population. Are we allowed to discuss this fact and decide whether or not to take the risk ourselves? Isn't this the process of informed consent?

We must have conversations about corruption. As with anything, there has been corruption and bribery and coverup at the highest government and corporate levels around vaccines in just the past few years. How can we have better transparency? Better oversight? How can we ensure the health and well-being of our families, communities, nations and world?

Please, we beg you, as we (society) have these conversations, have an open mind and an open heart. We can find answers together if we commit to dialogue and fact-finding. But we must remain committed to civility, committed to loving one another as co-beings on this journey. Let's find our answers together. After all, we're all one big creation together.

CHAPTER 19

Consumer Products

"Pick your poisons wisely and cautiously."

-Doc Love

None of the consumer products that we buy at a store (or online) would be around if we were placed on this Earth, no cities, no cars, no roads. Therefore, we have to use discretion and discernment as we choose products for ourselves and our homes.

Beginning with our personal hygiene, there are natural alternatives to every mainstream product. You may have to try more than one to find a good, effective, natural substitute. A great example of this is deodorant. Most commercial deodorants contain aluminum, which is a toxin, and has been implicated in several disease processes, including breast cancer (in men and women). You may have to try a half dozen natural deodorants before you find the one that works for you. We know that we did. But, it's worth it.

There are ample natural toothpastes out there. You will have to find the one that you like best and decide whether or not you want it to contain fluoride, another toxin. As with deodorants, you may have to try several.

Other products, like shampoos and body washes, should be examined for how natural they are. If they contain things like sodium laurel sulfate, you may want to replace them with a more natural option. For your hand soaps, you will have to decide whether you want them to be antibacterial or not (remember our microbiome).

Ladies, if you use makeup, can you switch to a more natural, mineral-based product? When you think about the toxic load impact of something that you put on your body every day of your life, you realize how that adds up over time. When it comes to feminine hygiene products, such as pads and tampons, can you find an organic, non-chlorine-based option? How about a DivaCup?

Detergents, dyes, and fabric softeners are also common culprits of illness in the family. Commercial detergents and softeners have been shown to be directly related to lung conditions such as asthma.

For all of these products, can you replace them with an essential-oil based product? There are companies, such as DoTerra, who specialize in creating natural, effective essential-oil based products for the home and body. They are third-party tested for quality and safety.

What materials are your clothes made of? Can you move in the direction of organic materials? Your clothing rubs against your skin all day, every day, and your skin can absorb toxins, detergents, and chemicals directly from the material.

Ladies, this especially important for your underwear, where these things can be directly absorbed into your bloodstream.

Home-building materials and chemicals are some of the worst offenders in toxic load accumulation. Carpet is one of the worst off-gassing materials known to man. Many building materials and chemicals are highly toxic. Using high-quality, HEPA air filters, and changing them regularly, will help to decrease this load in your home, although our highest recommendation goes to purchasing an air-purifying machine for your home and/or office. One breath of "normal" air in today's society contains more pollutants than our ancestors would have been exposed to in their entire lifetimes.

Food storage is a relatively new thing in the history of humanity. ZipLock bags and plastic containers are very convenient, but highly toxic. If you are going to use tupperware, glass is the best option.

CHAPTER 20

Wisdom from Symptoms

"Thank you for this lesson."-You to the Universe

Your Source-given design comes with its own on-board warning system. It is a highly advanced, intelligent detection and biofeedback system. Almost every sensation you will ever experience is actually there for your feedback and your wellbeing. Every pain has a purpose and if we listen, pay attention, and process, then react appropriately, our health will flourish. Put on your Secret-Formula-Glasses and examine some of these common examples:

- Fever – Fever is your friend. When your body is exposed to bacteria or to a virus, it will raise your core temperature in order to denature (kill) that threat for your survival. Ideally, you want to help a fever as much as you can. Get adjusted, stay hydrated and sweat. It is your body's natural defense mechanism and you want it to work. Each time you interfere with this process by doing things to decrease the fever, you are causing your body extra work and likely prolonging the infection.

Discuss with your doctor what safe levels of fever are. If at any time you or a loved one cannot hold down or take in water, or become delirious, immediately seek emergency medical attention.

- A runny nose – A runny nose indicates that your body is trying to eliminate particles or allergens inhaled or digested that are toxic or poisonous to you. You don't want to stop a runny nose, you want it to do its job efficiently and effectively.

- Headache – A headache is most often a sign of another underlying condition. You are not designed to have headaches and you are not built deficient in Advil or Tylenol. The most common condition underlying a headache is dehydration. The second most common is stress. When you have a headache, that is your body's way of telling you to slow down and make changes, whether in your nervous system mode, nerve supply or environment.

- Digestive Pains – Most people's gut health is a wreck. In our natural environment and Source-given design, the first time we experience a stomach ache or reflux or heartburn or bloating or gas-we would take note of what we ate and that it made us feel that way and not eat it again, or not in such quantity. The problem here is that many of us are "used" to having digestive issues and covering them up with Tums or Mylanta or Pepto Bismol. When you are having digestive problems of any sort, it is your body's check-engine light going off to clue you in to your nerve supply, what you are consuming and/or the state of your gut health.

- Constipation – If you can't poop-YOU HAVE A PROBLEM. And your body is telling you. If you need laxatives or softeners, same thing. This is a sign from your body to check your hydration, your nerve supply and what you are eating. Chances are that one of the above are not in keeping with your Source-given design.

There are loads of other examples. Indeed, almost every symptom has a lesson to teach us about our environment, or our life and the way we are living it. When you understand holism and vitalism, you want to help the body run its processes, not reduce its symptom(s). If the check engine light on your car is on, would you cover it up with a piece of tape or get it checked out to find the solution? Every symptom is a check-engine light. Sometimes the answer is as simple as hydrate or check the nerve supply. But just like with your car, the longer you wait and the more you cover it up, the more expensive and invasive the solution becomes.

CHAPTER 21

Now That You Know....

"Knowing is half of the battle." – G.I. Joe

You have been given the Secret of Life. You are now one of the all-time, great, sacred truth-keepers. The application of this information will lead to unbelievable levels of health, wellness, and vitality. It is your Source-given birthright.

This book is a treasure trove of information as seen through the lens of The Secret of Life. It is highly unlikely that you will be able to apply it all at once and live it perfectly, so pre-emptively give yourself some grace. Know now, before you even start, that perfection is not the goal. Incorporating this information, just one piece at a time, is a major win each time. The more pieces you can easily incorporate into your life concurrently, the sweeter your life experience will be.

You now have in your possession a sacred trust. Given to you, as it has been given to us. Guard it well. And, share it freely.

"Do all the good you can.

By all the means you can.

In all the ways you can.

In all the places you can.

At all the times you can.

To all the people you can.

As long as ever you can."

– John Wesley

Printed in the United States
By Bookmasters

Printed in the United States
By Bookmasters